The b

Bosworth

1485

Stephen Lark

Website - www.BretwaldaBooks.com
Twitter - @Bretwaldabooks
Facebook - Bretwalda Books
Blog - bretwaldabooks.blogspot.co.uk/

First Published 2013
Text Copyright © Stephen Lark 2013
Photos, maps and illustrations Copyright © Bretwalda Books 2013, unless otherwise stated
Drawings by Leanne Goodall and Darren Bennett.
Stephen Lark asserts his moral rights to be regarded as the author of this work.
All rights reserved. No reproduction of any part of this publication
is permitted without the prior written permission of the publisher:

Bretwalda Books
Unit 8, Fir Tree Close, Epsom,
Surrey KT17 3LD
info@BretwaldaBooks.com
www.BretwaldaBooks.com
ISBN 978-1-909099-86-9

CONTENTS

CHAPTER 1
THE WARS OF THE ROSES

The vicious dynastic conflict known to us as the Wars of the Roses tore England apart between 1455 and 1497. Although there were prolonged periods of peace within the wars, this was a period of violence, bloodshed and lawlessness such as England had not seen since the reign of King Stephen in the 12th century.

Historians have sought to link the wars to various social trends within England, to underlying economic factors and to religion. However, there can be little doubt that the prime cause of all the trouble was King Henry VI. Not that this was really his fault. Henry was a weak and simple man who suffered bouts of mental incapacity that came and went with startling suddenness. He would sit down to dinner, fall into a trance and not recover his sense for hours, days or weeks on end. Nobody knew when the next bout would strike nor how long it would last. What was clear was that there were unscrupulous men and women close to Henry who were only too willing to take advantage of his weakness and bouts of insanity for their own purposes.

Richard Duke of York was a very different character. Even his friends did not claim he was particularly clever, but he was honest, diligent and brave. He was, moreover, cousin to the king and due to the complex history of the Plantagenet dynasty had a claim to the throne every bit as good as that of Henry himself.

In 1453 Henry fell into a stupor more prolonged than before. A Council of Regency was set up with York as Lord Protector. York promptly reformed the government, throwing out the more corrupt of Henry's favorites. When Henry regained his senses in , those favourites were back in power and moved to have York arrested and executed on trumped up charges. In 1459 York gathered his men for war, sparking the Wars of the Roses that followed.

For the next 12 years England was torn apart by warfare as the rival claimants to the throne slogged it out, backed by powerful magnates who were often following their own agendas and ambitions. By 1471 the noble families of

4

England had been decimated as bloody battles were followed by murderous show trials, ad hoc executions and secret assassinations. York himself was killed, so was Henry VI along with a clutch of dukes and earls, plus thousands of lesser men. Emerging triumphant from the carnage was York's eldest surviving son, King Edward IV. Edward was supported by his younger brother Richard, Duke of Gloucester. Edward also had two sons, also Edward and Richard, to be his heirs.

The new Yorkist dynasty seemed secure, while the rival Lancastrian faction - named from the fact that King Henry VI had been the grandson of the Duke of Lancaster - was utterly destroyed. Henry and his son were both dead the Lancastrian nobles in exile, hiding or reconciled to the handsome, urbane and politically astute Edward IV.

But then it all went wrong. Edward IV died suddenly in 1483 at the age of only 41. His eldest son, Edward, was proclaimed king. But before the boy could be crowned it emerged that the marriage of his parents had been invalid under Church law, so he was illegitimate and unable to inherit the crown.

That left the boy's uncle, Richard, the only surviving male heir. He became king as King Richard III. However, some of Edward IV's most loyal supporter suspected that Richard had fabricated the evidence against the marriage and, in due course, thought he might have murdered Edward's two sons. Unrest began to fester against the new king, especially among those nobles who found him to be just a bit too honest and diligent at rooting out corruption for their tastes.

The true heir to the Lancastrian claim to the crown of England was King Joao of Portugal, but living in France was a second claimant. Henry Tudor had only the faintest claim to the throne. He was the great great great grandson of Edward III by way of John of Gaunt's illegitimate children by his beautiful mistress Katherine Swynford. Gaunt had later married Swynford and persuaded the Church to retrospectively make his children by her legitimate so that they could inherit his wealth. They were, however, specifically banned from inheriting any titles, including that of King of England. Nevertheless, Henry Tudor now claimed that very title for himself.

As yet Tudor had no chance of becoming king. But as unrest against Richard grew, Tudor decided his time had come. In 1485 he invaded England.

CHAPTER 2
THE MARCH TO BOSWORTH

Henry Tudor sailed from Harfleur with about twenty ships and landed at Milford Haven, where the Cleddau rivers meet, on 7 August 1485 and two dramatic weeks followed. He had been expected to arrive during autumn 1483, during the "Buckingham Rebellion" but that revolt had fared badly and he was advised to remain in Brittany and then France for a while.

By this time, Tudor already declared himself to be the rightful King, citing several ancient bardic prophecies, some of them spurious. Some exiled

The quayside of Harfleur, then a busy port, in Normandy from which Henry Tudor set sail. (Vigneron)

Lancastrian peers and knights accompanied him but the bulk of his original retinue consisted of French and Swiss mercenaries, the latter being expert pikemen, numbering about half of the four thousand total. Sir Richard Corbet, among his band, had rescued him at the Battle of Edgecote in 1469 before Jasper had sent him to Breton exile. He was also accompanied by Bernard Andre, a lawyer, Augustinian friar and poet from Toulouse. Andre was to play no part in the battle because of his clerical status and because he was almost certainly blind. Another non-combatant was Reynold (or Reginald) Bray, who had also known Tudor since 1469 before serving Lord Stanley and then Lord Hastings. He was involved in one of the 1483 rebellions but was pardoned for all his offences in early January after which he laid the financial groundwork for the invasion, as recorded by Vergil.

Apart from being a big opportunity to emphasise his quarter-Welsh ancestry, Milford Haven was far from the most obvious place to launch an invasion. William of Normandy had landed at Pevensey Bay in Sussex and the south or east coasts have always been easier to reach from the continent. There are reports that Francis, Viscount Lovell was at Southampton, which may have deterred Tudor from landing on the south coast. Lovell's subsequent movements in seeking sanctuary suggests that he must have reached Leicestershire in time for the battle.

A further problem for Tudor was that William Herbert, Earl of Huntingdon, remained loyal to Richard. Herbert, whose family name was previously ap Tomos, was married to the King's illegitimate daughter Katherine and received an annuity of six hundred pounds – then a massive sum. Now he prepared to defend his South Wales estates whilst sending a message to Richard about the invasion – ironically he was based at Raglan where Tudor had been his father's ward.

Herbert's role in the campaign has been controversial. He promised to aid Richard, but wasn't at Bosworth two weeks later. Although he was born only the year before Richard, Herbert had become Earl of Pembroke in 1469, at his father's execution after Edgecote, before exchanging the title a decade later for that of Huntingdon. He was appointed Chief Justice of South Wales in the wake of the Buckingham rebellion and was a great-grandson of Dafydd Gam, the principal Welsh hero of Azincourt. There had been something of a power vacuum in Wales after the fall of Buckingham, who had a castle at Brecon where his son Edward Stafford was born.

Henry Tudor was delayed and diverted even further, marching through mid- and north Wales, although it allowed him to recruit more Welshmen. The Stanley

7

affiliation in Clwyd, based at Holt, also attracted support. Tudor wrote his main "commission of array" from Machynlleth and crossed into England at Oswestry, before moving on to Shrewsbury, Stafford and Warwickshire. In passing from Knowle to Coventry, he seems to have diverted via Merevale Hall on the 13th, although the reason for this is not clear.

Henry spent the eve of the battle at Atherstone, a day to which he later gave a special significance. By then, his own force had grown to about five thousand, with Gilbert Talbot and Rhys ap Tomos supplying the additional numbers. In that era, Coventry was far more prominent as a centre of administration while Birmingham was yet to truly come into existence.

The old town square at Atherstone. On the night before the battle Henry Tudor found lodgings in a house in the town while his army camped in the square and in fields nearby.

King Joao II of Portugal was the legitimate heir to the Lancastrian claim to the English throne. He was, however, content with his own realm. To ensure that this line of descent was brought into his own, Richard had arranged to marry Joao's sister Juana. The marriage had not yet taken place when Henry Tudor landed in Wales, declaring himself to be the true heir to the Lancastrian claim and so King of England.

Given the Tudor tendency to edit the historical record in their favour, reports of the conduct of the Stanley brothers during the preparation and battle must be treated with caution. This is especially so as in 1495 Sir William Stanley betrayed Henry by declaring for the pretender Perkin Warbeck, with dire consequences for himself. What the two were in fact up to can be deduced by a comparison between Lord Stanley's uncommitted approach to fighting battles and Sir William's consistently enthusiastic approach, a comparison that dates back to Blore Heath in 1459 when Sir William fought on the Yorkist side, but his brother halted his troops six miles from the battlefield and played no active role.

Sources tend to suggest that it was Sir William who met Tudor at Stone whilst Lord Stanley merely asked Richard's permission to return to the family estate at Lathom. His son George, Baron Strange, took his place at court. George held this title, despite his father being only a Baron at this stage, by virtue of his marriage.

When he heard that Tudor had landed, Richard's immediate reaction would have been that this was the invasion attempt he had hoped for and feared, in almost equal measure, since Buckingham's rebellion fizzled out. There was sure to be a battle and it might result in his defeat and death but it might also result in a victory with "Tydder" captured, killed or in flight – the second outcome meaning that the last quasi-Lancastrian boil would have been lanced.

9

The ruins of Berkhamstead Castle, Buckinghamshire. Richard left his mother here for the last time as he set off on his fatal last journey. (Stephen McKay)

The "Lancastrian claim" should have devolved properly on Joao II of Portugal, a king disinterested in invading England. To neutralise this claim, Richard was preparing to marry Joao's sister Juana. The second wedding at this ceremony was to have been that of Edward IV's daughter Elizabeth to an authentic Lancastrian noble. If this had taken place before Henry Tudor could land it would have limited his plans for he was widely thought to be keen to marry Elizabeth himself.

The campaign was also welcome to Richard as it was to be his opportunity to lead the fighting in his own battle, not just supporting Edward at Barnet or commanding through delegated powers at Picquigny or Edinburgh but echoing his father's ultimate authority over his campaigns.

The King's status as a childless widower was reminiscent of that of Richard II and he would have been painfully aware of this. Nevertheless, his large grants to Queen's College, Cambridge, in 1484, as in 1477, are powerful evidence of his love for his first wife Anne Neville, whose part in this story is sadly limited, but they are likely to have met over twenty years earlier at the estate of her father (Warwick) where he was a page. His boar badge is now adapted for that of Queens' College (note the mobile apostrophe) although Henry VII duly reversed the grants.

Richard was that summer, on a formal royal progress around England, having departed his mother's residence at Berkhamstead for the last time. He had reached

Nottingham when he heard the news of Tudor. About this time his private correspondence with his sister in Burgundy probably ceased. Certainly, Richard's extant patent rolls end on August 9th and it has been suggested that his clerks were thereafter busy mustering troops, although subsequent documents could have been lost.

Richard declared Sir William Stanley a traitor and had little expectation of support from Sir William's brother, Lord Stanley, who was moreover Tudor's stepfather. He knew that the de Veres (Earls of Oxford) had long fought in the Lancastrian interest, the previous Earl and his eldest son having been executed in 1462. He could, therefore, discount support from the present Earl, who had led the Lancastrian right at Barnet, escaped to Scotland, tried to land at St. Osyth in Essex, been attainted and imprisoned in Calais before escaping again and joining Tudor's exile in Brittany only the previous year, his mother having been under house arrest for some thirteen years. Richard might have expected support from the Earl of Northumberland, who had supported his claim but his Neville connections and Edward IV's earlier actions may have alienated his Percy sensibilities.

Richard could definitely rely on John de la Pole, Earl of Lincoln and the eldest son of his sister Elizabeth, Duchess of Suffolk. Richard's own son had died, Edward's sons were in hiding or dead and Clarence's son was excluded by attainder but Lincoln was a steadfast supporter of his uncle, following him in authority over the north and being regarded as Richard's heir, officially or not. He was the first to bear the formal title "Lord President of the Council of the North", heading a body that survived until 1641.

Richard could also rely upon the veteran John Duke of Norfolk, Sir Robert Brackenbury, Viscount Lovell, Sir Richard Ratcliffe and the lawyer Sir William Catesby, the latter two being from gentry families. Lovell's military experience went back to Edward IV's first victory at Towton and Ratcliffe's to the second at Barnet. Brackenbury was a Durham man who had been Treasurer of Richard's household. He was now Constable of the Tower, visiting Calais earlier that year before being entrusted with the defence of the capital, but travelled to join his King on 20 August.

Richard's only "invisible general" was the Bishop of Bath and Wells, Robert Stillington, a former Keeper of the Privy Seal and Lord Chancellor, who had exposed Edward IV's illegal marriage two summers ago.

The emergency was now on and Richard's other plans, whether of remarriage

11

or Crusade to recover Constantinople (now Istanbul) that had fallen to the Turks in his infancy (an intention declared to von Poppelau and echoed through two small figures in a subsequent portrait), would have to wait.

Did he make a grievous error in failing to pursue the invaders earlier? Might an attempted invasion the previous year have been easier to deal with? Perhaps he underestimated the total force that would be arrayed against him by the time it reached the Midlands. Perhaps he didn't expect to have enough troops ready to advance into Wales, or imagined that Huntingdon, Lovell or Brackenbury could deal with the problem completely and not merely delay it. This point has been discussed for five hundred years and will be on many more occasions. Some of the mercenaries supplied by Charles VIII of France, through his sister and Regent Anne of Beaujeau, included a Scots contingent.

The battle monument at the Bosworth Heritage Centre stands on top of Ambion Hill, where Richard's army almost certainly camped the night before the battle.

Richard was not alone in international terms either. Whilst a French King would consider it part of his job description to destabilise England, the Habsburgs were uneasy at the threat of French influence growing too large and the Emperor Maximilian had delegated the great Spanish warrior Juan de Salazar to remain in England, to advise and aid the King. We are indebted to de Salazar for a unique insight into Richard's mind just before the battle – it is through him, von Poppelau and the Scottish ambassador Archibald Whitelaw that we have the best unvarnished descriptions of him.

Troops were raised from the East Midland counties and a large contingent left York on 20 August. There are persistent rumours of a preliminary skirmish happening that day with Sheriff Boughton (of Leicestershire and Warwickshire), John Kebell of Rearsby and four men of similar status ("tenants-in-chief") being killed. This tradition might also be attributable to a transcription error or an obvious desire by their families to avoid attainder but we can be sure that they didn't suffer simultaneous fatal coronaries. The others (Coke, Curson, Hampden and Joyce), have been claimed as adherents of Oxford, as they were from Suffolk and North Essex within fifty miles of his Castle Hedingham base, and thus of Tudor.

If these rumours hold water, the skirmish could have involved Stanley forces intercepting troops trying to join the royal army, but other historians have cast doubt on this as they could have been Norfolk's men. Towns and villages like Halesworth and Brightwell, where William Joyce and William Curson lived, are surely too far from Castle Hedingham and Curson had served with Norfolk, whose estates extended as far south as Colchester, in 1484. For whatever reason, these six "Inquisitions Post Mortem" gave 20 or 21 August as the men's date of death.

The royal army also included troops from the South-west, East Anglia and the North although commissioners could not recruit men as quickly for defence as they could for an invasion. In theory, it was about half as large again as Tudor's but the usual factors of terrain, tactics and numbers were joined by the great unknown of loyalty. Richard had ordered the Stanley brothers to raise troops in Cheshire and Lancashire and they may have managed up to ten thousand between them although he had obvious reservations about the allegiance of such a force by then. Approximately three quarters of his men would have been archers.

CHAPTER 3
MEN, WEAPONS AND TACTICS

The armies of the Wars of the Roses were raised in three basic ways. First there were the town and county militias, second were the retainers of the various noblemen and third were mercenaries, mostly foreigners. The size of the armies involved has provoked a lot of dispute. Contemporary chroniclers had not, by and large, been anywhere near the fighting since most of them were monks or clerics. They recorded figures of anything between 20,000 and 80,000 men for the armies involved, but this was probably based more on guesswork than anything else. Modern historians have tended to reduce these numbers substantially, suggesting that most armies were around 10,000 to 15,000 strong

This archer is typical of the period. Because large numbers of archers served on both sides he is wearing fairly substantial armour to provide protection against incoming arrows. He has a mail shirt reaching to elbows and knees. Over this he wears a sleeveless jack made of up to 22 layers of linen over which are stitched plates of iron or horn. His sallet-style helmet is of steel, padded with wool. His lower arms are free to allow him to draw his bow. The lower legs are unarmoured, probably to allow him to move nimbly around the battlefield. His bow is the standard longbow of the period and he has a quiver of arrows at his belt. His sword and buckler are for hand to hand fighting.

with the largest army fielded at this date being the 35,000 Lancastrians who fought at Towton in 1461.

In the context of the Wars of the Roses, the fact that the provision of armed men was in the hands of nobles and knights has been used by some historians to suggest that armies could be raised quickly for anyone who could pay.

The men in the armies consisted of various types: heavily armoured infantry, archers, more lightly armoured cavalry (hobilars) and a number of more specialist soldiers. The armoured infantry were drawn up between four and eight ranks deep. The men stood shoulder to shoulder to form a solid block of men. A high proportion of these men were armed with pole weapons of one sort or another.

Standing on the flanks of the densely packed armoured infantry were bodies of archers. By the Wars of the Roses archers were not as effective as they had been. New types of armour took the form of steel plates shaped to wrap around the body. The plate armour was also designed to have smooth shapes and flowing profiles so that an arrow would glance off it more easily. Even so the new armour was not entirely proof against arrows. Given the huge numbers of arrows shot during battles at this period some at least would find a weak spot and penetrate to the man's flesh.

This fully armoured knight wears the very latest and finest armour, so he must be a rich man. The body is entirely encased in plates of quality steel shaped to fit the individual. Pieces of mail are used to give added protection at joints. His main weapon is a poleaxe, with a long sword as a secondary weapon. This sort of armour was surprisingly light and flexible, allowing the wearer freedom of movement.

A new factor by the time of the Wars of the Roses was the advent of guns. These came in two forms: handguns and artillery. For the most part these made relatively little impact on tactical dispositions on the battlefield. Hand guns increased the death rate in the last few yards before the men got to work with hand weapons, while artillery increased the number of deaths at a distance. However, neither were so deadly as to alter the dispositions or tactical formations. The bigger guns rendered useless the old stone walled castles, one reason why sieges were relatively rare in the Wars of the Roses.

Although heavily armoured, mounted knights had fallen out of use there was still a role for horsemen. These hobilars - also known as currours or prickers - were more lightly armed than knights and rode less expensive horses. Their roles were mostly off the battlefield. They scouted ahead and to the flanks of the army looking for the enemy. They rode ahead to secure bridges or fords. They rode off to carry messages to other commanders or to local authorities. They sought good campsites, bought - or in France stole - food supplies.

During the Wars of the Roses it was customary for an army to be divided into three "battles". Each battle consisted of a mix of soldier types, with archers and men at arms. The commander of the army usually took command of the central battle, with his more experienced subordinate leading the foreward battle and the third commander the rear battle. Any artillery present was usually kept with the central battle, as much for its commercial value as its use in fighting. Hobilars or other mounted troops would usually be formed outside this traditional structure. They would have their own commander answerable to the army commander, but would only rarely be actually with the army itself. More often the bulk of these men were off on detached duties of one kind or another, though rarely more than a day or two's ride from the army.

It was traditional for the central battle to be the largest, perhaps as strong as the other two put together. Some commanders preferred to vary this arrangement. The most usual variation was to increase the strength of the advance battle to make it capable of independent action. Some army commanders even preferred to put themselves in charge of the advance battle, delegating the central battle to the third in command.

Armies tended to be commanded by the most politically important nobleman present. It tended to be these men who had called the army into existence and who decided what its purpose was to be. There were usually professional soldiers present, but their role seems to have been to offer advice when asked for it.

Chapter 4
The Commanders at Bosworth

Richard III was born in 1452 while his father was still Duke of York. He was the youngest of four sons at the time and had little expectation of becoming King. Together with his brother George, Richard was sent to safety on the continent as the battles became more frequent in 1459-60. They returned in 1461 after their father and brother Edmund had been killed at Wakefield but their brother Edward Earl of March had been crowned as King Edward IV after his great victory at the Battle of Towton. Edward made George Duke of Clarence and Richard Duke of Gloucester. As the decade progressed, Richard remained staunchly loyal to Edward, but George joined the Earl of Warwick's rebellion in 1470 which briefly restored Henry VI.

Richard excelled himself at the battles of Barnet and Tewkesbury the following year, as Warwick was killed and Henry VI died soon afterwards. Edward was restored and his three sons were born at this time. The elder boys, Edward and Richard, would outlive him, but the youngest, George Duke of Bedford, died after about a year. Clarence was pardoned, though he was never again really trusted by Edward or Richard. In 1478, in circumstances that are still controversial, George was arrested and hurriedly executed, after which – an Act of Attainder was passed, barring his descendants from the throne.

Richard was sent to France to fight a war that ended only when Edward signed a treaty with Louis XI. He was next sent to rule northern England from his estate at Middleham and married Anne, daughter of Warwick, just as George had married her sister Isobel. Richard and Anne had one known child, Edward, although Anne may have been pregnant on other occasions.

As commander in the north, Richard had the job of invading Scotland in 1482. Although this had mixed results, he took Edinburgh almost bloodlessly and Stanley conquered Berwick. Richard had already formed a fearsome reputation, not seriously hampered by whatever physical infirmities he may have had.

England was stunned by Edward's early death the following year. Richard was

17

named as Regent and Lord Protector to Edward's eldest son Edward, but at this point Edward's secret pre-contract of marriage to Lady Eleanor Butler was revealed. Edward IV's children were thus illegitimate and unable to reign. A Parliamentary assembly petitioned Richard to take the throne and he did. Lord Hastings tried to organise a coup, but was foiled and executed by Richard. Rather more serious was a rebellion led by the Duke of Buckingham that autumn, but again Richard thwarted his enemies. .

No sooner did he appear secure on the throne than Richard suffered two devastating blows. His son died in 1484 and his wife became terminally ill a few weeks after that Christmas. She died on 16 March, most probably of cancer or tuberculosis. Richard sought to deal with his vulnerability as a widower by marrying Juana of Portugal, sister of King Joao and by now a senior member of

King Richard III as shown in a contemporary portrait. This painting was retouched after his death to emphasise his hunched back, but is otherwise considered to be a reasonably good likeness. At this date portrait painting was in its early days as an art form.

the true Lancastrian line. Fourteen days after Anne's suffering ended, Sir Edward Brampton was in Portugal, the country of his birth as it happens, to negotiate this marriage. It was agreed that Richard's eldest illegitimate niece, Elizabeth, was to marry Joao's cousin Manoel. Elizabeth was the eldest daughter of Edward IV and was aged 19 at this date.

So, as Richard prepared to tackle the Tudor challenge, a brighter future with a second marriage and possibly more children appeared to be on his horizon.

Henry Tudor was born in 1457, a few months after his father Edmund had died. Edmund was the elder son of Owen Tudor, a Lancastrian servant who had possibly married Catherine de Valois, the widow of Henry V, before being beheaded after the battle of Mortimer's Cross in 1461. His mother was Margaret Beaufort, daughter of a Duke of Somerset. The Beauforts were the illegitimate children of John of Gaunt, legitimised by Richard II but barred from the throne. Margaret married four times but Henry's traumatic birth when she was only twelve rendered her infertile thereafter.

The surname Tudor is today rendered as Twdwr in Modern Welsh, but was given in several contemporary documents as "Tydder". The name ultimately derived from Theodore.

In 1462 Henry was sent into exile in Brittany, a duchy not on friendly terms with the French crown and remained there for his own safety. His father's stepbrother, Henry VI, had conferred the Earldom of Richmond (in Yorkshire, not Surrey) upon Edmund Tudor and Henry subsequently used this title although his grandfather's execution and attainder for treason meant the title was invalid.

King Louis XI died in 1483, a few months after Edward IV, and Henry was not going to be welcome in France for much longer. A French proclamation exists describing him as the "younger son of Henry VI", although it is unclear whether that false claim originated from Henry or Louis. That same year Henry tried to involve himself in the Buckingham rebellion, withdrawing just in time when it failed. He joined his uncle Jasper Tudor, who was still claiming his forfeited title as Earl of Pembroke. That December, Henry promised to marry Elizabeth, Edward IV's eldest legitimate daughter, and prepared for an invasion.

Milford Haven is far from the obvious landing point from France, however Henry was emphasising his Welsh ancestry. In fact, he had only one Welsh grandparent, one French and two English.

King Henry VII depicted a few years after Bosworth, by which time he was entitled to wear the royal fur of ermine. This distinctive fur of white with black flecks is taken from the winter coat of the stoat, which is white with a black tip to the tail. The fur is dense, soft and luxurious which is why under medieval sumptuary laws it was reserved to royalty.

Thomas, 2nd Baron Stanley was born in about 1435, the eldest son of Henry VI's Comptroller from an important family in Cheshire and Lancaster who were descended from Edward I. Thomas' father died in 1459, and he was summoned by the Lancastrian commanders to the battle of Blore Heath that year. His men stopped a few miles short of the battlefield, possibly because his brother was fighting for the Yorkist cause. He did turn up at the Battle of Northampton the following year and take part. Some historians place him at Towton now fighting in the Yorkist interest as Edward IV acceded. Stanley was Chief Justice of Chester and Flint by this stage and his half-hearted commitment was to continue during the Warwick Rebellion of 1470-71. As Warwick fled through Cheshire in 1470, Stanley failed to support him, possibly deterred by the presence of an army led by Richard, Duke of Gloucester.

Edward IV returned and tried Stanley but no punishment followed. Stanley missed the battles of Barnet and Tewkesbury but served in France in 1475 before joining Gloucester in the Scottish invasion of 1482. He showed unfamiliar commitment as his troops captured Berwick whilst Gloucester raided further north.

Although he did appear loyal, there were some problems. Stanley and Gloucester had an ongoing dispute over the ownership of the valuable Hornby estate. Moreover, Stanley had been suspected of being involved in Hastings' plot but there had been no real evidence of his complicity and had merely been placed under house arrest for a while. In 1472/3 he had become Lady Margaret Beaufort's fourth husband, despite her vow of chastity, and therefore Henry Tudor's second stepfather, which divided his loyalties. On his accession, Richard made Stanley a Knight of the Garter and Steward of the Household. After Buckingham's execution, Stanley succeeded him as Constable of England and was given custody of his wife.

At Bosworth, Stanley's son Lord Strange was a hostage to Richard for his father's conduct. Odd as it may sound, this may have been Stanley's idea.

Sir William Stanley was Thomas' younger brother, though his precise date of birth is unclear. Unlike Thomas the perpetual bystander, he garnered a reputation as a military commander. He fought for York at Blore Heath and Tewkesbury, capturing Margaret of Anjou at the latter, being knighted and made Chief Justice of North Wales as a reward. He had fewer differences with Richard than did Thomas and was given some of Buckingham's estates in North Wales when that Duke's rebellion failed. However, his loyalty had always been to Edward IV not to Richard of Gloucester. In 1485 he came to believe that Edward's sons, the "Princes in the Tower" were dead and blamed Richard. He was later to be persuaded of the opposite and acted accordingly regardless of the consequences for himself - though in 1485 that lay in the future.

By summer, he was very clearly disgruntled with Richard's regime, more openly than his brother. He actually met Tudor two days before the battle and Richard proclaimed him a traitor.

Sir John Howard, 1st Duke of Norfolk was also descended from Edward I, his family holding the additional title of Earl Marshal which required them to officiate at coronations and a state openings of Parliament. John was a veteran by the time of Bosworth, being at least 60. Like Richard, he had had at first little expectation that his title would devolve upon him. His grandfather Thomas Mowbray was raised to the Duchy in 1397 but died two years later and four more generations of Mowbrays held it. The third married Lady Elizabeth Talbot, sister of Edward IV's first wife, but they had only a daughter Anne. She married Edward IV's younger son, Richard of Shrewsbury, and died the last of the Mowbrays at nine. John's mother Margaret had married Sir Robert Howard and so John effectively inherited the title from his cousin's grandson-in-law.

John Howard's first battle had been against the French at Castillon in 1453. He served in several "Roses" battles under his cousin, the 3rd Mowbray Duke, being knighted after Towton as Edward IV was crowned. As an additional reward, he was created Sheriff of Norfolk and sought sanctuary in Colchester during the Warwick Rebellion of 1470-71, from which he emerged as Lord Howard to fight at Barnet and Tewkesbury. During the Scottish campaign of 1481-2, he commanded the English fleet.

Apart from these five, there were arguably two "invisible" but prominent generals. Lady Margaret Beaufort was born in 1443 and married four times but her vow of chastity made the last one a political transaction. John Morton was born in 1420 and became a lawyer and fervent Lancastrian supporter, proscribed after Towton but reconciled with Edward IV on his return. He was made Master of the Rolls and Bishop of Ely.

Both played a critical role during Richard's Protectorate and reign. Morton was involved in the Hastings plot and imprisoned under the care of the Duke of Buckingham at Brecknock and is thought to have manipulated the latter into revolting. Lady Margaret was also involved in fomenting this rebellion, probably in the hope that either Richard or Buckingham would eliminate the other but be weakened in the process, clearing the field for her son. Arguably, this is exactly what was to happen.

Chapter 5
The Battle of Bosworth

Those troops that intended to fight gathered near Market Bosworth, each army accompanied by two heralds in their distinctive tabards. This was particularly appropriate as Richard had officially founded the College of Heralds the previous year, under the authority of Norfolk, to supervise the use of heraldic devices and the genealogy of those entitled to bear arms. Some historians, led by Anne Curry, Professor of Medieval History at Southampton University, now believes that the site was mutually agreed. This might sound bizarre to modern ears, but was not unknown in medieval times. Mustering an army and keeping it in the field was no mean feat, so commanders often needed to fight a decisive action quickly. Arranging a date and field of battle that gave neither side an obvious advantage was one way to do this.

Richard's last evening was spent near Sutton Cheney and the invaders' camp was at Atherstone. Many soldiers, on both sides, now wrote their wills and these would include Norfolk's man Thomas Longe. For those who died and were attainted, such a will would prove irrelevant as their property would pass to the Crown.

This is also significant because Henry later compensated those from Merevale and several other villages en route whose crops were damaged by his army's marching and fighting during the harvest season. Some of his troops may also have pilfered crops to eat on the march, before fighting. Those who know anything about Henry VII, as he was to end the month, will not expect him to have compensated anyone without good reason.

Much has been said about Richard III's character over the years but two psychologists from Leicester University have spoken at a Richard III Society Conference recently. Professor Mark Lansdale and Dr. Julian Boon first examined the two-dimensional calculating Shakespearean monster but concluded that Richard's loyalty to his family makes this highly improbable. They add that his disability, such as it was in life, would not have affected his character. Given the power that devolved upon him so suddenly, they believe that he was "intolerant of uncertainty", giving him a set of moral standards, a strong belief in the law and justice, with a "black and white" view of the world. His legislation and his conduct right up to the end of the battle give much weight to this.

In common with much of Richard's life and reign, the Battle of Bosworth has probably attracted more myths than any other of its type or era but we can now be sure of a few facts about it. There are some accounts on which we can rely more than others.

We have known for many years that the battle took place within a few miles of

St James's Church in Sutton Cheney. The church now bills itself as "The Battle Church". It is thought that King Richard heard mass here just after dawn on the day of the battle, along with many of his men and commanders.

Leicester - and that the site lay somewhere near Market Bosworth was universally agreed for centuries. The name "Battle of Bosworth" was first used by Fabyan not long afterwards, although Redemore Plain was another name used at the time.

Two alternatives for the precise site have been suggested since then. One of these, suggested by Michael Jones (Psychology of a Battle: Bosworth 1485), would place it about eight miles west, closer to Dadlington (near Coventry). He also lined up the armies at different angles. Indeed, some bodies were subsequently found there and a chantry built for them in 1511, although they could have died after fleeing several miles. In any case, the Dadlington sites do not fit well with the battle's name.

Fenn Lane southwest of Sutton Cheney. Richard and his army would have marched down this old Roman Road before fanning out to either side of the road to take up battle formation and block Henry's advance.

Identification of the site has been complicated by Glenn Foard's findings of ordnance, but no arrowheads, at the edge of the traditional venue. This is possibly because the soil is relatively acidic in the area, meaning that metal detectors are consequently set in such a way as to avoid smaller iron products. We know that artillery were being used in battles of this period, as were smaller hand held guns, but the long bow remained the key missile weapon among English armies.

It is the recent discovery of Richard's badge of a gilded silver boar, together with the tip of a highly ornate sword that has surely clinched the argument. Most battlefield historians now believe that the scenario put forward by Peter Hammond in his 2010 narrative is the most convincing, although Jones was one of the first to place pikes at the scene and has a very useful insight. Interestingly, both believed that Richard's body was lost.

The battle can now be confirmed to have taken place along Fenn Lane, about a mile and a half southwest of Ambion Hill, now thought to have been where Richard's army camped the night before the battle. It also appears that the King's army advanced first so that fighting took place approximately where Tudor's army lined up.

We know that the site and alignment of the opposing forces makes the terrain a critical factor because of the proximity of hills and marshland but also the direction of the sun - especially important for archery. There are no reports of adverse weather on August 22 so; depending upon the time of day that the battle started or finished one army may have been hampered by facing the sun although a long battle may have seen this disadvantage change. Think how often you have seen a goalkeeper wearing a cap in such conditions.

We know that this was Henry Tudor's first battle but Oxford was an experienced general to make up for this. By contrast, Richard had fought at Barnet and Tewkesbury in 1471 and the invasion of Scotland. Through his charismatic "command by example" style adopted from previous commanders, he would have been expected to prevail, had all other factors been equal.

We do know that certain people were not present. Huntingdon (Richard's son-in-law) had "played his part" by forcing Tudor to turn north. It may have taken too long for him to reach Leicestershire. Sir Edward Brompton, the Portuguese Jewish convert and Sir James Tyrrell of Gipping Hall in Suffolk, were the King's men. Tyrrell was his Master of Horse and High Sheriff of Cornwall, but was in France. Brompton, a former Bailiff of Guernsey and godson to Edward IV, was probably engaged in other urgent business.

Although we do now know the battle site, other things remain obscure. Several stories dating from some years after the battle are well known, but should probably be dismissed as unsafe legends. These include:

Richard is supposed to have banged his spurs against Bow Bridge when leaving Leicester, and his head to have done the same on the way back (the latter supposedly predicted by a local woman).

Richard's "sleepless night" (recorded by Vergil and the Crowland continuator) and "failure to celebrate mass" (supposedly caused by nightmares resulting from non-existent crimes) – do generals who subsequently lose battles never have an opportunity to pray with their army first?

The village of Fenny Drayton, east of Atherstone, was on the route of Henry Tudor's army. The village suffered much damage at the hands of the Tudor army and Henry was later forced to pay extensive compensation to the villagers.

"Dickon's Well" from which he is supposed to have slaked his thirst during the battle (despite not being that active until his fatal charge) and a host of other misleading "place names". Though to be fair his army may have collected water from here, some of which could have reached Richard.

Giving the battle an alternative name being to fit Thomas the Rhymer's fourteenth-century prophecies of a set of battles. This includes the creation of a fictional village of "Sandeford" in the Leicester-Coventry corridor for Bosworth and "Gladsmuir" for Barnet, but these names were little connected with the "Wars of the Roses" until the Victorian era.

A message supposedly posted on Norfolk's tent: "Jockey of Norfolk be not so bold, for Dickon thy master is bought and sold" (the current "transcription"). If it existed, it would not deter this veteran, who had fought for York thirty years earlier as a commoner and then a knight. Could a Tudor spy really have reached the midst of the royal camp with its leaders always at least semi-alert?

That the crown was found in a hawthorn bush, and it became a "Tudor symbol".

The folklore now includes two ballads: "of Bosworth Field" and "of the Lady Bessy", which are also of dubious accuracy.

The general problem with these myths is that few were reported at the time, some surface through More and Shakespeare, others beginning as late as three centuries later. Vergil in particular seems to repeat the Azincourt story, including the absence of a chaplain to the (defeated) French army there.

We must even be careful with the estimated numbers in each army, whether through propaganda or the inclusion of the disloyal. It was, curiously, easier to raise troops to invade than to resist an invasion, as shown at Agincourt, because the latter were not generally paid. We need to remember that Richard was not yet thirty-three, much younger than his subsequent portrayals in literature and art. We also need to avoid looking at Henry VII as he became: the middle-aged founder of a relatively secure dynasty but instead to see him as he was in 1485 - a desperate, inexperienced opportunist who was the last chance for several long-term Lancastrian supporters. We are not watching the stability of the Lancastrian or pre-1399 era being restored through God's judgement but we are watching "a damn close run thing", as Wellington said of Waterloo, in which neither leader dictates the course of events more than the other.

Sunrise that East Midland morning would have greeted Richard, presumably still in Sutton Cheney, at about five. There was no point in rising later and finding the enemy in a more advantageous position. His priests were not bound by the

28

same urgency, but a crucifix and staff have been found by archaeologists on the battlefield indicating that they did make it to the scene of action in time.

After eating and celebrating Mass, his army would have proceeded along Fenn Lane to the battlefield by Ambion Hill, from the east north-east. Adopting a possibly Burgundian tactic, they formed a line about a mile long to avoid being outflanked, with Norfolk leading the archers and the King himself the vanguard. Brackenbury was with him, in charge of the household troops and mobile guns brought from the Tower whilst Northumberland was on the left. Richard had a strong interest in guns, having commanded two men (William Cloake and John Brambrough) to build some guns, supply them to the Tower and provide powder in late 1483.

Walter Devereux, Baron Ferrers was another Yorkist veteran, having first fought at Towton twenty-four years earlier and then been a commissioner of array in the

The battlefield looking north from Fenn Lane towards Richard's initial position. Ambion Hill is just out of view to the right.

The view southwest from Richard's initial position toward Crown Hill (just to the right of the spire of Stoke Golding Church. He would have seen the colourful banners of the Stanley armies drawn up there as the battle began.

West Country – his descendants included the Elizabethan and Civil War Earls of Essex. Richard's troops, with a captain for every hundred men, would have worn a livery collar with his own badge, in contrast to Tudor's adoption of the Lancastrian generic "SS" badge. Some members of both armies would have worn polished, decorated and even gilded armour.

The royal standard bearer was very probably Sir Percival Thirlwall of Northumberland, Although Sir William Parker of Devon and Gilbert Swinburne of West Swinburn also in Northumberland have also been suggested for this role, every unit of a hundred or more had its own, smaller, standard. Some cavalry at the sides would be there to deter desertion. The marsh, now known as Fenn Hole with Redemore Dyke flowing into it, would have been to the left of the royal army, almost between the forces. It was in this area that the spent ammunition was found.

An army of this era was invariably accompanied by heralds and Richard's was known as "Blanc Sanglier" ("White Boar"), who had been his ducal herald. Hammond has putatively identified him as the son of Sir John More, the Norroy ("north country", starting from the Trent) King of Arms, although this is disputed. Heralds were primarily observers with a sort of diplomatic immunity and Blanc Sanglier had a sad duty to fulfil afterwards as Henry had no further need for his services. Indeed, he attainted one herald - if this was Blanc Sanglier, he is believed to have lived on for about six years.

It is likely that Richard's army was awaiting their enemy by seven o'clock and one of their principal objectives was to block Tudor's road to London, whether in victory or in flight. The possibility that both King and claimant could be killed or mortally wounded was conceivable. Richard had probably already donned a special harness (or "German Gothic" armour) adapted for his scoliosis and skin-tight almost like a modern rugby jersey. Additionally, most writers portray Richard as now putting on an armoured helmet with a small crown attached. This was ceremonial but was also for the purpose of identification, a double-edged sword as it was to turn out. He had seen the Stanleys taking up position on the nearby Crown Hill to the south, remembered their long dispute with the Harringtons over the Hornby estate, and adjusted his plans accordingly.

Richard had more trust in the Earl of Northumberland, who had presided at the trial that sent Earl Rivers, Richard Grey and Sir Thomas Vaughan to the block for treason in April 1483. However this trust may have been misplaced since the Earl failed to initiate an attack as Lord Stanley was sited near him. Sir William Stanley was further embedded in the Tudor contingent.

Henry Tudor and his allies would have travelled some three miles south-easterly from Atherstone along Watling Street, into the early sun, before turning left to take their places with Oxford on the left. Reverting to type, Lord Stanley evidently declined the opportunity to command the rebels' vanguard, opting to join the battle later. John, Lord Welles, half-uncle of Tudor and from another Lancastrian family, was joined by Robert Morton, nephew of the notorious Bishop, and Sir Edward Woodville among the challenger's force. Woodville, a sailor, is scarcely mentioned in the records before his brother-in-law Edward IV's death but had fled to Brittany with many of the royal jewels. The story is complicated because another Robert Morton, a squire from Yorkshire, fought for Richard.

31

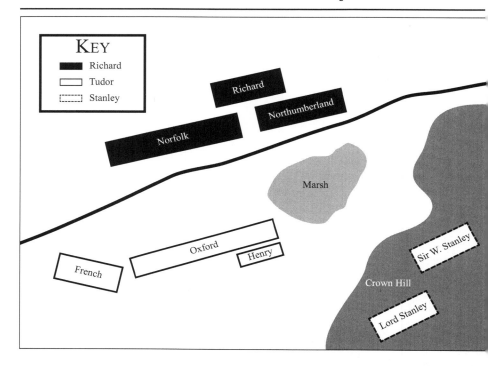

The precise positions of the armies when the battle began is still disputed. It seems likely that main bodies were as shown here with Richard's army north of what is now Fenn Lane and Henry's to the south. The two Stanley armies are known to have been on Crown Hill, though which was where is unclear.

In anticipation of victory and the pre-dating of his reign, "Richmond" illegally knighted several followers including his standard-bearer, William Brandon, a distant cousin of the Earl of Lincoln. His standard, the undifferenced royal arms was a naked claim to the throne of England. It also meant that both armies would, confusingly, be under the same flag.

Talbot joined Oxford on the right, the latter leading the archers, whilst Savage and Tudor himself led the left. They were also accompanied by the Richmond and Windsor Heralds. The former was Roger Machado who had sailed with Tudor after spending many years in Portugal, his apparent country of birth.

Recent historians have suggested that the battle began at about eight and was

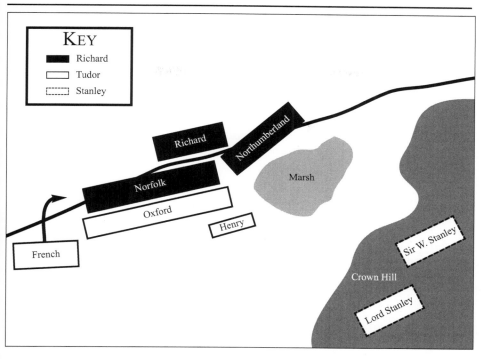

Richard ordered his men forward to engage Henry Tudor's. The marsh blocked Northumberland's route, but also served to shield Richard's army from those of the Stanley brothers. Norfolk's flank was exposed, so the French moved forward to attack this vulnerable sector.

over by noon or just afterwards. During this time, the sun would have been almost behind Richard's army at first, swinging round almost to the perpendicular, although "wheeling" during the battle could have complicated things further. By arriving first, he had the earlier opportunity to determine the angle at which the armies engaged. He could have chosen a different angle and followed a more regular strategy, blocking the road to London more effectively. He seems to have erred uncharacteristically, although Sir William Stanley's troops were in his line of sight and on his mind.

Another legend has it that, on seeing Lord Stanley's banner ranged against the anointed King, Richard is said to have ordered that Strange be beheaded but this never came about. This could have been caused by the time pressure or the fear of reprisals from Strange's step-brother, but there are few authentic sources for this and we could be looking at just another legend. It is quite possible that Lord Stanley was out of sight at that time and the execution order was never given.

The armies, who may have started as much as half a mile apart, now both advanced and the royal artillery took aim at Oxford's right flank, as did their bowmen. Oxford and the French-Scottish mercenaries, commanded by Philibert de Chandee, mostly avoided the shot and attacked in a wedge-shape, reinforced by pikes and under covering fire – from archers and the likes of a rough-cast bronze hand cannon, fragments of which have been found behind Tudor lines. The royal army was ill-prepared for the presence of pikes and there was some panic among Norfolk's contingent. This was exacerbated when someone, reported to be Savage, killed the Duke. One of the ballads, but no other source, puts this near Dadlington windmill, about a mile from the principal action.

The only account of the battle we have from one of Richard's supporters is that from de Salazar, to Ferdinand and Isabella, and he reports that Richard was determined "to win or die as King". In this way, just as both armies retreated a little from the beginning of the encounter, the King sought to change the course of the battle with a dramatic cavalry charge, having already spotted his challenger. This bold tactic, practiced at other battles before and since (Jones lists de Montfort at Evesham, Henry V's brother Thomas of Clarence at Bauge, Richard's own father at Wakefield and Ferdinand of Aragon at Toro, where de Salazar had also fought), would have been conclusive had it worked, as Tudor would surely have fled, leaving his force without a leader or a purpose. It was hampered as many of Northumberland's men failed to join in, although had they advanced, the royal defensive line would have been broken. Jones reminds us that just as many of Tudor's troops failed to engage, except the mercenaries. A letter from one of these mercenaries, a Frenchman, is still extant. It describes Richard's entire cavalry division, numbering about a thousand, on the charge and that it only failed due to a defensive technique recently developed by the Swiss. At the Battle of the Spurs, some thirty years later, a veteran of Richard's army talked Henry VIII out of a similar charge.

Richard rounded the marsh and Northumberland's wing and approached Tudor's elite guards, first killing Brandon (the knight of a few hours standing), throwing the titanic Midlander Sir John Cheyne from his horse and coming very close to his challenger. In this charge, he was joined by a few hundred of his elite

The Battle of Bosworth 1485 and the Burial of King Richard III

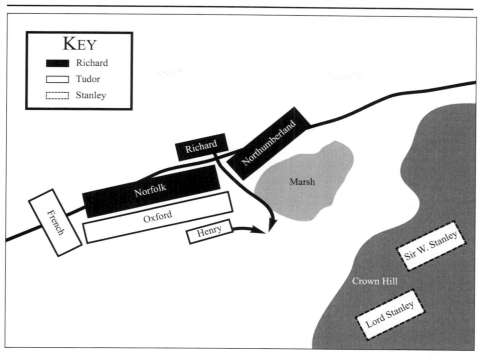

As Norfolk held off both the French and Oxford, Henry and his retinue began riding toward Crown Hill, presumably to seek to persuade the Stanley's to join the battle. Richard saw the move and charged forward with his own bodyguard in an effort to kill Henry and so end the battle, and the campaign.

knights including Brackenbury, proving more reliable than their other commanders. Only the French and Swiss mercenaries blocked his way, guarding Tudor with their long pikes but they couldn't fully repel the royal cavalry. Horses do have an instinct for self-preservation and can be deterred by eighteen-foot poles with spikes.

Now Sir William Stanley's men came forward, having seen Tudor in peril. Richard was urged to flee but flight had never been part of his chivalric style and he fully decorated his armour before resuming the charge, on a second horse if his first had indeed been lost. Even Polydore Vergil, one of the most servile Tudor chroniclers, is forced to admit that Richard "alone was killed fighting manfully in the thickest press of his enemies". The life of this great warrior and last Plantagenet King ended as he sustained several simultaneous blows whilst on the ground – a life that might otherwise have ended peacefully in his beloved North had Edward's reign not unravelled so dramatically. He who dealt the ultimate fatal blow remains unidentified. Rhys ap Tomos is suspected by most, such as Guto'r Glyn who told of him "shaving the King's skull" but one Rudyard of Staffordshire also claimed responsibility. Jones tells us that Richard was more like his father than any of his brothers were, in build, appearance and approach to life. Both seem to have been admirers of the Roman general Stilicho, who served in England and died (by beheading) on 22 August (408).

Much of the royal army then did attempt to flee, with mixed results, but Northumberland's unit then stood firm, having defected by pre-arrangement. Some of the remainder escaped, back towards Sutton Cheney or due south, but others were killed or captured and many surrendered. Henry then attainted these men on charges of treason, something that came as a considerable shock. The captives and their surviving relatives lodged immediate appeals, but Henry was intransigent. An explanation for Lord Stanley's passive conduct is that he could, had Richard won, have been better placed to argue for Sir William's life if he was not himself seen as a traitor.

So ended the Battle of Bosworth. Richard III, the reluctant King, was dead. For the second and final time in the second millennium, a King of England had died in battle and this King was a descendant of the first, Harold II, via the royal houses of Hungary, Naples and France to Edward III. Whitelaw said of Richard that "never has so much spirit or greater virtue reigned in such a small body" and he was greatly mourned in York, as its civic records show.

The average subject would not have felt an immediate difference and there were no simplistic "You are now leaving the Middle Ages" signs in every village. The modern view is that the medieval era in England lasted beyond Henry's reign into the Reformation. However, some of Richard's most enlightened legislation was reversed and the Tudors claimed responsibility for the rest. Tudor historians went on to claim that their House made England a more stable realm but that was based upon the sheer good fortune of its founder at Bosworth and the subsequent ruthlessness of his dynasty.

The Yeoman Warders were founded later in 1485, replete with the newly invented badge of the "Tudor Rose", to guard the sovereign. The secret Court of

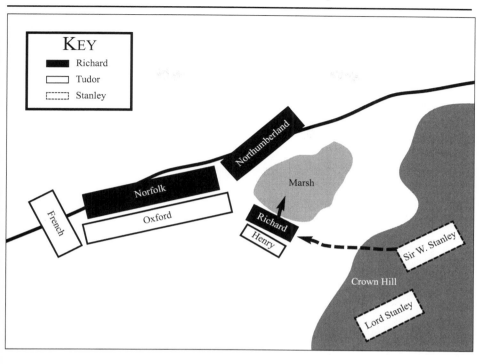

Seeing Richard and Henry both isolated with their relatively small bodyguard's Sir William Stanley launched his own men forwards to take Richard in the flank. Richard and his me were forced back into the marsh, where they were surrounded and killed.

Star Chamber followed two years later and Poynings' Law suborned the law of Ireland to the English Parliament in 1495. Tudor monarchs asked to be called "Your Majesty", not "Your Grace" as had their predecessors. The heresy laws of Henry IV (de heretico comburendo) were then re-imposed – Henry VII being recorded as debating theology with one prisoner before allowing his fire to be lit. In the next reign, noblewomen found themselves for the first time exposed to the laws of treason. Generally, England became a far more centralised state.

The "crown" (a coronet from Richard's helmet) appears to have been presented to Tudor by a Stanley brother (probably Sir William) and he became Henry VII but the hawthorn bush in which it was thought to have been found is probably illusory as large scale enclosures leading to the growth of such bushes only happened centuries later. Only later still was a hawthorn bush logo associated with Henry and the crown had probably been hidden by a looter. Talbot and ap Tomos could now be knighted for real and Henry could spend a few peaceful weeks at Woking with his mother, Lady Margaret. As his, largely foreign, troops marched on London, an unprecedented outbreak of sweating sickness struck the capital, killing two Mayors and some aldermen within a week. The two were inexorably connected by some.

Henry's war on Richard's kingdom ended but a war on his reputation was just beginning. It began with him leaving the battlefield as would a dead traitor, supposedly no longer King that morning and with many of his books (his "Book of Hours" for instance) and other possessions passing to Henry and his family. When he landed, Henry acted as though Richard was not a valid King but was to need his predecessor's legacy a decade later, during the "Perkin" rebellion.

The propaganda war escalated after 1509. It ended, after Henry's son and grandchildren had died, in Shakespeare's grotesque pantomime villain to which actors such as Garrick and Cibber added their own detail. This narrative began to unravel, however, through Sir George Buck, writing just after Shakespeare.

What of the other participants, in the battle and the background? In an unprecedented act, Henry proclaimed that he had become King on 21 August, before the battle, and that those who opposed him the following day were committing high treason. In the quarter of a century that I have read about Bosworth and the events before and afterwards, only two writers have sought to condone this and Henry's first Parliament approved this reluctantly. Not the least of their reasons was because a subsequent successful rebel could have followed the precedent and attainted anyone who fought for Henry.

Norfolk, Brackenbury, Ferrers and Ratcliffe were among the dead and were attainted, Norfolk's son (Thomas, Earl of Surrey) not being confirmed as Duke for nearly thirty years, after his service at Flodden. Sir William Catesby was captured and hanged three days after the battle, possibly to silence him and make it easier to suppress Edward's marriage pre-contract. There were so few executions that week that he must have been singled out as there were some 30 attainders, including those already dead. Robert Catesby, of the Gunpowder Plot, who was shot in 1605 whilst resisting arrest, was his direct descendent.

Lincoln served Henry for a year and a half before joining the Simnel rebellion and dying at Stoke Field but his view of Simnel, to whom he would have ceded

38

precedence, is not recorded. His other adult brother, Edward, was Archdeacon of Richmond and seems not to have been at Bosworth, although he had probably died by October 1485. Francis, Viscount Lovell escaped to sanctuary in Colchester, where he was briefly joined by Humphrey and Thomas: the Stafford brothers of Grafton, distant cousins of the Dukes of Buckingham. The Staffords revolted within the year and Humphrey - who had destroyed the Anglo-Welsh bridges in 1483, trapping Buckingham in the Principality during his rebellion - was executed. Lovell was last seen at Stoke Field, although a safe conduct for him to Scotland in 1488 has been found. Thirlwall, "fighting on after his legs had been cut from under him" and Swinburne both fell although Parker lived to 1510 and Jane, the ill-fated Viscountess Rochford, was his granddaughter.

The new King's stepfather, Baron Stanley, was raised to the Earldom of Derby and Constable of England. He died peacefully in 1504, months after his son Lord Strange who Richard failed to execute at Bosworth. Sir William was not further honoured and his correspondence during the "Perkin" rebellion included a pledge not to raise arms against a man who could have been Edward IV's younger son. He was prosecuted for this and executed in 1495 - some sources subsequently made Lord Stanley into the hero of Bosworth instead. The Earl of Oxford commanded the vanguard again at Stoke Field and at Blackheath against the Cornish rebels. He was made Constable of the Tower and Lord High Chamberlain before dying in 1513, childless by both his marriages. Bray was also handsomely rewarded, becoming Chancellor of the Duchy of Lancaster and Under-Treasurer of the Exchequer along with judicial offices and stewardships. He was knighted on 28 October, at the coronation, again after 1497 and again in 1501 before dying childless two years later with a curious reputation as an architect.

Chandee was created Earl of Bath in January 1486 but returned to Brittany and died as early as that year, evidently without a legitimate male heir. Northumberland also served at Stoke Field but was less fortunate as he was sent to collect taxes in North Yorkshire during 1489 when a mob, furious at his betrayal of Richard, killed him. Bernard Andre went on to become a tutor to both Henry VII's surviving sons as well as his authorised biographer. He played his part in the Tudor propaganda machine and is, curiously, regarded by some as an eye-witness to the battle and subsequent events. Tyrrell was recalled and executed for treasonous correspondence with the Earl of Suffolk in 1502 after serving as Governor of Guisnes, although rumours of his "confession" post-date Henry's reign, More being first to mention it. Brampton went into exile, where he was

recorded as meeting "Perkin", before dying in 1508. Cecily, Dowager Duchess of York, died in 1495, survived by only two of her twelve children. Bishop Stillington was imprisoned, with one interval, until his death in 1491.

Bishop John Morton became Archbishop of Canterbury and a Cardinal before dying in 1500. William Herbert of Huntingdon was described as a widower when he attended Elizabeth's coronation so Katherine is likely to have died by 1487 – he died in 1491, leaving only a daughter by a previous marriage. Sir Edward Woodville was made captain of the Isle of Wight during which he visited Spain. In 1488 he sailed to Brittany to fight the French at St. Aubin, where he was killed. Juana is supposed to have learned of Richard's death in a dream – she retired to a convent at Aveiro and died in 1490 – but Manoel, Duke of Beja, became King of Portugal. Charles, son of (Sir) William Brandon, was created Duke of Suffolk in 1514 but his family forfeited the title forty years later. Roger Machado became Clarenceux King of Arms, the senior provincial position supervising England and Wales, dying in 1510. Edward Stafford, aged seven at the time of battle, was restored to the Duchy of Buckingham by November 1485 and opposed the Cornish rebels in 1497 but was executed in 1521.

Henry VII developed a reputation for parsimony and continued to attaint people without always executing them. His Titulus Regius ("The Title of the King") repealed Richard's Act by the same name which was destroyed and thought lost until a copy turned up. As a consequence, Elizabeth of York was re-legitimised, Henry marrying her in 1486. To intentionally further the "Son of Prophecy" concept, their first child was born at the Wessex capital of Winchester the next year and named Arthur. Only then was she crowned.

Lord Welles was raised to a Viscountcy and married to Elizabeth's sister Cecilia, whose previous Scrope union was forcibly annulled. Henry also married his cousin Richard Pole, who he knighted, to Lady Margaret Plantagenet, daughter of the Duke of Clarence and thus another of Richard's nieces. Henry made sure that there would be no legitimate grandchildren of Richard III's brothers than through his own close family.

Facing page: The traditional end of the battle as Henry Tudor knelt on the field of battle to be crowned by Lord Stanley with Richard's discarded coronet. The event is supposed to have taken place on top of Crown Hill, an area now largely covered by a 20th century extension to Stoke Golding village.

CHAPTER 7
THE BURIAL AND DISCOVERY
OF RICHARD III

At the conclusion of the battle, Richard's body was first led, by his Blanc Sanglier herald on a horse, to the Newarke, one of the Leicester churches. The body was exposed for all to see for some days as it was important that an ex-King could be seen to have died. The passing of this time also allows rigor mortis to finish, making the burial easier. A plaque that I viewed almost every day for three years marks a city centre bridge that he would have crossed. The body was then placed into the custody of the Grey Friars and provision was made for a respectful, but not lavish, burial in the choir of their church, a place of honour about fourteen miles from the battlefield.

So might the story have ended, except for the disappearance of important documents and the development of several increasingly hostile chronicles, culminating in Shakespeare's play. The real tragedy is that anyone credits this as more than just a very good drama.

The grave may have been marginally too short, posthumously exacerbating his spinal condition but August 1485 is likely to have been a hot month. An alternative explanation I have read is that bodies were routinely buried with the head slightly raised as if on a pillow. His original tomb is said to have been of alabaster, bearing an effigy and a poem that was recorded for posterity. There was no shroud available as it seems that the friars would expect to be buried in their robes.

Many of his family also died violently: John de la Pole, Earl of Lincoln (nephew, Battle of Stoke 1487); John of Gloucester (illegitimate son, executed c.1499); Edward, Earl of Warwick (nephew, executed 1499; Edmund de la Pole, Earl of Suffolk (nephew, executed 1513); Lord Richard de la Pole (nephew, Battle of Pavia 1525, whilst in exile); Henry Pole, Baron Montagu (great-nephew, executed 1538/9); Margaret Pole, Countess of Salisbury (niece, executed 1541)

The Grey Friars council offices, built on the site of the old Herrick House, itself built on the site of Greyfriars Church. The burial was found in the car part at the rear of this building. (Robin Leicester)

and Henry Pole the Younger (great-great-nephew, disappeared in the Tower 1542) – all feeling the consequences of Tudor insecurity.

Richard was, therefore, treated well in death by his immediate successor. Henry's demise and his son's marital indecision had serious consequences for other deceased monarchs and nobles as Henry VIII and Cromwell set out to destroy the monasteries and friaries that had been a source of opposition to the Reformation, as well as the depositories of much property. Alfred the Great, for instance, is known to have been buried in Winchester but his body awaits rediscovery.

Greyfriars in Leicester was eventually dissolved and rumours were spread about the fate of Richard's body. It was said that his remains had been thrown into the neighbouring River Soar. A stone coffin that local cattle were using as a trough was said to have been his, although it had been made several centuries earlier. The site of Greyfriars then passed into the hands of Robert Herrick, a local craftsman and Mayor of Leicester.

Many years after Alderman Herrick's time, the land passed into the use of Leicestershire County Council's Social Services, where it entered use as a car park. Meanwhile, two individuals, both prominent members of the Richard III Society, began a search for the body. Philippa Langley set out to determine the location of the "Greyfriars Warrior" from the existing historical records, knowing that she had only one realistic chance to find him, whilst Dr. John Ashdown-Hill sought to confirm some comparable DNA that he had collected for a previous, inconclusive, search for Richard's sister Margaret (Duchess of Burgundy) in Mechelen, Belgium. Without the detailed planning of these particular individuals, some others and the fundraising, enthusiasm and insight of the Society as a whole, this stunning achievement may not have been possible.

Both of these tasks took several years and the latter involved some scientific analysis as well as a sample from a living individual. DNA analysis dates back about thirty years and divides into mitochondrial DNA (inherited through the female line and very useful) and nuclear DNA (from all ancestors but not of so much use yet), although the latter includes the Y-chromosome (male line only and quite useful). The other advantage of female line descent is the relative certainty it gives over descent through the male line.

From Richard's sister, Anne Duchess of Exeter, through women including the wife of William Wilberforce, a seventeenth generation female line descendant – Michael Ibsen from Canada, whose late mother Joy Brown was the original donor – had been traced and his mtDNA is now proven to be a perfect match. In any case, mtDNA had been taken from a second, anonymous, collateral descendant, although this was to prove unnecessary. The University's archaeological team had little expectation of finding a monarch, one of them (Richard Buckley) pledging to eat his hat if they did. Looking for a particular individual and finding them is almost unprecedented in these cases.

The date of 25 August 2012 fell three days after the 527th Bosworth anniversary and on the same anniversary of Catesby's execution. Following agreement from the University of Leicester, Channel Four TV and the Ministry of Justice (as required under exhumation law), the excavation began. One of the very first finds was a male body which had scoliosis of the spine and severe head injuries consistent with having been sustained in battle.

44

The excavation ended just in time for a press conference on 4 February, the day after Candlemas. Despite the presence of artillery at Bosworth, the only item between the Warrior's bones was a nail although the lack of a coffin suggests that it could have been much older, even Roman. A female skeleton was also found, presumably associated with the Church, but she was re-interred in the original place as the exhumation licence didn't cover her.

The press conference was able to report that the Greyfriars Warrior's mitochondrial DNA was identical to that of Michael Ibsen, showing that they

The burial site of King Richard III in Leicester, photographed in September 2012 when the archaeological excavations were still continuing. At this point the identity of the remains had not been identified, hence the ambiguous nature of the sign. The king's bones were discovered at the bottom left of this photo. (Chris Tweed)

45

have the same female line ancestors. This mtDNA is of an exceptionally rare habloid (J1C2C) type, borne by only 1-2% of the population of Europe. He had died of several head and torso wounds from swords, axes and halberds in the late fifteenth or early sixteenth century at the age of about thirty, having a high status in life with a lot of seafood in his diet. Given all this and the position of the body, in what was the church choir, it was determined that the Warrior could only be Richard III. None of the wounds had healed so they must all have been suffered at or soon after the time of death.

Although the exhumation may have damaged his skull further, experts went on to reveal a reconstruction of his face. It shows Richard to have had "gracile" features and reminds us that he died at thirty-two. Hostile sources, here including More and Shakespeare, have described him as up to a decade older, to be committing "war crimes" when he was an eight year-old in Burgundian exile. He is routinely played by much older actors, just as portraits were "adapted" to add wrinkles and uneven shoulders, as Pamela Tudor-Craig first claimed nearly forty years ago. By adding his known hairstyle and clothes, we now know almost exactly how Richard III would have appeared to a time-traveller with a camera

The results also bury some of the myths about Richard. Whilst More wrote about a "withered arm", displayed at the council meeting leading to Hastings' execution, there is no evidence of this. It is not credible that he could have ridden or wielded a sword so proficiently if he suffered in that way and his arms are shown to be of equal length. Professor Lin Foxhall, Head of the Archeological Department, tells us specifically that the "hunchback" (kyphosis) portrayed by Shakespeare and others is not present although he suffered from scoliosis, a relatively minor lateral spinal curvature and not at all visible when clothed. It was probably of adolescent onset, meaning that his bones and muscles had developed differently, particularly as he would have begun military training at this stage, thus using those muscles differently.

The extent to which this affected his life can be judged as follows: he married at about twenty and commanded armies from this date in France and Scotland. Before his marriage, one or both of his known illegitimate children had been born. We know this because John of Gloucester was Captain of Calais in 1485 and is unlikely to have been twelve or under and because Katherine was already married. Richard was evidently not serious hampered in horse riding or his private life, as also shown by the Portuguese remarriage negotiations. Fellow scoliosis sufferers include Usain Bolt, Michael Phelps (both of whom need to be careful with

46

analgesics), Princess Eugenie (she had an operation at an early age and her father is also Duke of York), the actress Isabella Rossellini and performer Toyah Wilcox.

His natural height was close to my own at 5ft 8in although the curvature would have reduced that by an inch or two. A friend now suffers from scoliosis and appeared to be two inches shorter than she would be, although she ran a marathon before first being afflicted. Other sufferers have written about the disease recently and they seem to live almost normal lives. One suggested that Richard's final charge, killing William Brandon and upending the large Sir John Cheyne is almost worthy of a Paralympic equestrian medal.

A German visitor to England in 1484, Nicholas von Poppelau, testified that Richard was several inches ("three fingers") taller than him and slimmer with delicate features but mentions no visible deformity, nor does any source before More. Von Poppelau was the owner of a heavy lance that many others had struggled to lift but Richard successfully raised it. He is also the witness to the grief Richard and Anne displayed at the death of their son Edward.

Richard's body now lacks feet but the centuries of building work around him will account for this. It has, despite the hostile rumours, survived much longer than those of his enemies such as Morton. So we can safely conclude that Richard's disability did not limit his everyday life or his prowess in battle. It would have been noticeable to nobody but his wife, earlier partners, mother and nurses, nor would he have shown pain outwardly or we can be certain that later "historians" would have commented on it.

Identifying Richard III is a great achievement in itself but it could also be a stepping stone to others. Many of Richard's relatives, whether in the female or male line, are as yet unidentified or not yet confirmed and he can be used for comparison. DNA analysis was, of course, discovered by Sir Alec Jeffreys at Leicester University and one of the early cases it solved involved the murders by Colin Pitchfork in Narborough, Leicestershire.

As time passes, the usefulness of the Y-chromosome for genetic analysis will surely increase and therefore it would be advisable to take and store some samples today, during the lifetimes of accessible and willing individuals. Richard's Y-chromosome has sampled and there are several relatives who could be traced through it. Just as I write, the Duke of Beaufort, in unbroken male line from Edward III through illegitimacy from the Dukes of Somerset, has finally made his Y-marker available. Last summer's dig in a car park could be just the beginning of something much greater.

Exhumation was permitted on condition that the Warrior is re-interred in Leicester Cathedral which will happen during 2014. The Richard III Society has designed a modest tomb in stone of a beige colour bearing St. Cuthbert's cross (for his piety), a white rose for his family and a white boar as his own symbol, for which it is now raising further money. He will be accompanied by a reconstruction of his crown in a tomb that will be partially produced by none other than Michael Ibsen. Richard will, once again, take a prominent place in the last city he ever saw, sharing the Cathedral with Thomas Wolsey, the Cardinal from my home town who didn't expect to die in Leicester either. A heart attack interrupted Wolsey's journey from York to London as he was summoned to answer charges of high treason.

Although Wolsey's lifetime comments on Richard were unfavourable, he was only about twelve at the time of Bosworth and we must understand the context of the repressive atmosphere that prevailed through much of the Tudor era. Strangely, I feel that they will enjoy each other's company, as victims of that atmosphere but whose reputations and bodies have long survived it.

Oh, and Leicestershire Social Services staff will be able to park again.

ALSO AVAILABLE IN THIS SERIES

The Battle of Wimbledon 568
The Battle of Lincoln 1141
The Battle of Chesterfield 1266
The Battle of Northampton 1460
The Battle of Losecoat Field 1470
The Battle of Bosworth 1485
The Sieges of Newark 1643-46
The Siege of Leicester 1645
More to come